GORGEOUS FREAK

Gorgeous Freak

Julie Poole

DEEP VELLUM PUBLISHING
DALLAS, TEXAS

Deep Vellum Publishing
3000 Commerce St., Dallas, Texas 75226
deepvellum.org · @deepvellum

Deep Vellum is a 501c3 nonprofit literary arts organization
founded in 2013 with the mission to bring
the world into conversation through literature.

Support for this publication has been provided in part by grants from the National Endowment
for the Arts, the Texas Commission on the Arts, the City of Dallas Office of Arts and Culture, the
Communities Foundation of Texas, and the Addy Foundation.

LIBRARY OF CONGRESS CATALOGING-IN-PUBLICATION DATA

Names: Poole, Julie, 1980- author.
Title: Gorgeous freak / Julie Poole.
Description: First edition. | Dallas, Texas : Deep Vellum Publishing, 2024.
Identifiers: LCCN 2023058327 (print) | LCCN 2023058328 (ebook) | ISBN
9781646053094 (trade paperback) | ISBN 9781646053247 (e-pub)
Subjects: LCGFT: Poetry.
Classification: LCC PS3616.O63727 G67 2024 (print) | LCC PS3616.O63727
(ebook) | DDC 811/.6--dc23/eng/20240105
LC record available at https://lccn.loc.gov/2023058327
LC ebook record available at https://lccn.loc.gov/2023058328

ISBN (paperback) 978-1-64605-309-4 | ISBN (Ebook) 978-1-64605-324-7

Cover design by Zoe Norvell

Interior layout and typesetting by KGT

PRINTED IN CANADA

To my future soulmate

Where the eff are u?

CONTENTS

Season: *Spring*

Season: *Summer*

Step <u>1</u> create a loving
    entity
Step <u>2</u> introduce yourself
   to this loving entity
Step <u>3</u> give this loving
   entity a name

Season: *Fall*

Creature two-hearts
I will admit I have no
 sufficient name for you
last night   I was
        writing poetry
in my dreams and got
hung up on a particular
  verb that I've since forgotten
My bladder was full
   and conducive to creative
      works   When I woke
        the line
   I thought was good
            was gone
            off on the back of an animal
         I picked mold off my morning
         bread and made a double strength
         cup of tea
            no paper
            to read
         I made due
            with a magazine
         but can't say that
      I registered what I read

Matador
if I play music
your voice
will leave me
The sun in the yard
hurts as much as
the dead roach's still-ticking
legs or the grackles
wading through grass
If I take off my shoes
it becomes harder to return
to the idea of going
somewhere
You know this
blood is
the color red
and ache
is the color
of afternoon
If no song
breaks
through to upset
day it becomes
too easy
to return
to bed

Pumpkin smell
I took myself for a second
walk and was accosted by
butterflies I met a new
type of bug
and screamed him off my stoop
accidentally
as his warrior's shell
unhinged itself two triangular legs
Like a large piece of ambling bark
he left the bench
where my roommate
set her houseplants
for sun-rehabilitation
I thought about calling
my mom but it was too
early to bother her
with my daughter-ness
Instead   I made my
bed to the best
of my ability
and listened to my
neighbors speak
in the yard

Loneliness
is a biscuit
even a dog doesn't want
I'm happy the couple
who took my table
were themselves overtook
by a conversation
they didn't want to
hear
We think we
own this world
but not even
a picnic table outside
gleaming
with   caterpillars
belongs to me
I took one up with
my pen after it
crawled on my
page and reared up
to say *Really*
that's what you
think of love?
When's the last time
you saw frogs
dance or watched the sun
come up over the moors?
Wait a second I thought
this is Texas   guy
& I can't tell your
ass from your face
but that
doesn't mean
that I don't want
you to live

Polygraph
   I woke fat with sadness
   it was difficult to walk
   I blinked open my neighborhood
   and saw a cat in the grass licking itself
   two boys jumping
  on a trampoline morning
  was misting confidently
no rain

leaves falling
  made my skin feel extra delicate
   I thought about my friend who'd died
    it didn't register at first
    but now weeks later a new feeling
    was hitting
    my body dumb

Or maybe it was allergies
   or the cute horrors of Halloween
    decorating the neighborhood
     or Christmas round the corner
     when her brother and mother
     would be without her
     I remember that particular cruelty
    when the crown of thorns Christ wore
no longer impressed me

Two blond ladies taunted me
   to stop at their garage sale
   Common you know you need
   something how true
   desire both problem
  and solution

Further on I saw two pairs of men's
shorts laid out on
someone's lawn for free
banished by the wife
of the household (cargos)

I went to a coffee shop
to forget my voice
sat next to a woman
writing holiday cards
until she too left me

When my friend's baby
   goes down that's
   when she'll call
  and we'll plan
     our lives   Heather
a smell I don't know but a
voice I do   My list
needs more famous
   moments
     and   exercise
      Her list needs
      a promotion and
    Fridays off with her son
   Goals I think
   are how we stop Death
who must think   *sheesh*
 you gals are boring
    We've   seen   loss
  rip right   through
  the trees from Washington
  to California
  To survive
  means making
  a check mark
   or filling in
  a box
  looking
to next month
to see what
went right
rejoicing

Gorgeous freak
bring me some
    apple sauce a digestible cloud
& 3 perfect tomatoes
    My mouth is purple
    from so much kissing
        I miss you   Alien
When will be this introduction
    we're to have   on the beach?
        I'll have two tin cans
                tied to my ankles
and a briefcase of lemons
    singing phrases
from my newest book
                    Mindfulness
implies a mind and breasts
    like watermelons
"that's impossible" says the stork
    about to deliver me
        your latest   love letter
        It's unsigned
but you've left me
    the crust from your
morning eye

Ghost
   how did the trees get so suddenly
   covered in lights?
   Fever seems a distant possibility
   and my friends are far
   Today I taught girls
   poetry & felt bad at it
   One said *A kid at my school*
   committed suicide   *Oh man* I said
   put that in a poem   No
   I didn't say that
    but put it in my own poem
    as I ate my complimentary
    sandwich under the eaves
  watching the peewee marathon
kick off in the rain
kids with numbers
 pinned to their chests
 tiny gold trophies
   for the 5 & 6 year olds
    that made it around the
    track the announcer
      under a tarp with
       a microphone charting their
       course to the finish line
       I will never be a parent
       Why did I just say that?
       The conference was
       for girls'
       empowerment
       & self-esteem
       I read them *Howl*
       and took out the
       following words

███
cock
balls
dick
and
pubic beard
Write you own Howl
A poem to define
  your generation
They looked at me like I was
nuts
      Someone said *Trump*
      Someone said *No way*
      Someone said *A boy*
      named Clark followed me
      around in the first grade
      and kept saying I love you I love you
      I love you
            Good write all
              that down
Ghost I am a bad teacher
I was afraid of them I imagined seven
different excuses for not showing up
I waited for the bus in the rain
wearing my role-model blazer
I walked down a winding road
to Austin High School
 to a room with only two faces
 waiting then a grand total of five
  How was I supposed to force them
   into the space of creation?
    One girl rolled her eyes Poetry
     is stupid feels like school
      Why did they come
        then when something
          more fun was just down
            the hall? Hip-hop dance

self-defense soapmaking
start you own small business
Write your Howl
If you don't
no one will
Put your little girl
cunts into it
It's Nov 5 2016
and we can't afford
to twirl our hair
We can't
afford to be
crushed by all
the things that
seem to
matter more
than us

Ghost
I remember
two sacred minutes
when they all seemed
to be writing the moment
so fragile I was afraid
to even look I stayed so still
so compact
so still
and tried
my best
to love them
through it

Fridays may not be
for love but they
are for writing
and reading
and poeting
They are for
a fortifying
  burrito
  & perhaps
an imported
  pineapple soda
They are for
  a peaceful shit
  while no one's home
  for the right
  to just look
  at the dishes
  How accidentally
  I've become
  myself today
  It's always a surprise
to have a face
and arms and legs
  and dreams
and this strong
  impulse to draw
  What treasures
will I find
  on my walk?
  The butterflies
are nearly gone
the blue ones
  especially

Now I only
find wet
things a baby's
sock I startle
Nobody's cat
off my lawn
Look! someone
just got a package
It's garbage day
and all the bins
are wonkily tossed
lids thrown open
poor smelly dears
I can always
tell who
the liberals are
by their bumper stickers
an old *Vote for Kerry*
seems particularly sad
& now I feel
less full than
that impossibly fat
spider who's made
its web in a strange
location between
a telephone pole
and a guy wire
Will we have
sidewalks soon?
Or will I be happy
to risk my life
at night walking
home in my clothes
of mourning
my wardrobe
more black

as time goes on
and my body
needs slimming
A moth
in the fall
is very much
like a flying
leaf though
I know that's not
a surprising thing
to say Look!
the sky is trying
to cry and I
just kicked
a cluster
of acorn hats

After an earwax
evacuation everything
   is loud
  and crisp
  the leaves
 my footfall
   the birds
      conversations
    the trickle
       of sprinklers
    It's like being
       naked
    The stream
      has a new
      music
      Friday
      traffic
      home
         The leaves
          are remarking
           loudly
            It's
           like being
            followed
        Maple leaves
        have a different
          sound from
         the ever plentiful
           small brown
           leaves that
            are eye-shaped
            maybe oak
         I assume everything
             that's not a maple

is an oak
This will be
a future
experiment
registering
the sounds
of dry
leaves as
distinct
as birdsong
Only you would
tell me
this isn't
stupid
Each day
I think
I know
nothing
& this is
a preferable
state
because
through you
I've taken
a new
interest
in the
world
I notice
but would've
ignored
that there are
nearly
20 different
leaf shapes
on the

ground
and I
could
only pick
out the
holly bush
and the
maple
I know 20
different
sodas
&
two
leafs

Season: *Winter*

Bird
  be confident
in me   I made
the   decision
to go buy
    apples

Honorary
practitioner
of anxious
   morning
      drink
      less
      caffeine
      Let your
         mind stutter
            open on
               its
               own
               terms
            then
         follow
         your
         feet
      outdoors
      Know simple
         morning
         hellos
      & that the pattern
         the cat
         wears
         is called
         tuxedo
            The small
               pup
               has no
               barks
               for me
               today
            until after

I've passed
the edge of
his   yard
and then
he remembers:
I was suppose
to bark!
bark
bark
More than
yesterday
I   feel I'm
falling
into this
day too
soon
already
one
noise
I wasn't
ready for
a Unicorn
Mover's
truck
Yes they
come to your
door and move
your fantasies
to Silicon Valley
or Los
Angeles
or Reno, Nevada
or NYC
anywhere there's
work
I run the opposite

direction
  of work
into simple
    sounds morning
into power lines
flecked with birds
  into the ripe smell of grass
  pushed by a
    leaf blower

Fog
I like
your quiet
unknowing mouth
We all sometimes
  feel we cannot
   see beyond
   the bridge
  of our nose
 but when
 a dog walker
  appears walking
    one
   then two
  dogs
    it's the gentlest
    sort of
     revelation

     Earth's magic
    leaves me
    dumb maybe
    I have to
     ignore it
     to live
    sanely
     at least
      because
     it's not
    sane
     to disrobe
      your puritan
       shirt

and titflash
    the perfectly
        blurred
        sun
        It's not
        sane to
        hear dove
        wings
        flap
        and
            shout
            I am
            in
                a   church
                right now!
                    I am in
                        a holy
                        state
                        of
                    non-
                    ambivalence!
                    Hurrah!

Transient light
I'm not
ready for
the cloaked
shapes
of evening

Love let me
be an idiot tonight
let me put panties
on my head
and pretend to sing
in the shower
I love the smell
of your
panties
the dog
does too
Hey wait
a second we don't
have a dog!
How did this
dog get here?
eating yours and
mines'
panties!
He's swallowed three pairs
already and you said
"Should we do something?"
And I said, "Let's just see
where this goes."
Now, where were we . . . Yes
I'd like to suggest
you take your dick out
and put it away
and take it out again
and put it away again
Now let's have a spelling contest
Marsupial
Mar soup ey al

Good now
You're the winner
of   a brand new
dog

Put a bow
  on the
  grass
it becomes
a present
  Put a
  turd
  on
  the
  side-
  walk
    it becomes
    an obstacle
    oops
    another
    obstacle
  Now
  where were
  we? Yes
  we were
    talking
    about
    love
  and how due
    to the rain
    the cacti
    have melted
    into sick
    soggy colors
      of green
  their
  points
  wilted

crowns w/ no
authority
That's politics
for you
a new man
moves
into
the White
House &
the things
of
nature
die

*

My landlord's
improving
the house
indication
I'll have to
move Yes
squalor
is a good
sign
but
exterior
paint
and
unsagging
a porch means
sayonara
I can live
with all
these strange
tufts
that fall out

43

of trees
I have a warm
hand-me-down
coat
and can sleep
under the
stars

*

Put a plate
in the dirt
it becomes
lunch
Put a cup
in the
bushes
it becomes
a coffee
date

*

We can all
agree that
a picture
of roses
is not the
same thing
as roses
that children
better
understand
the
value
of fun

*

If you took away
  my organic
  soups I'd still
survive on Campbell's
  Warhol
    knew Campbell's
    was acceptable
    fare
      I can still
    see him eating
  cheeseburger
        after cheeseburger
We've become
    far too
    delicate
    and
    precious
      about
      our
      modes

*

  Red berries
  shouting through
  green
  I stop to
  look at
  you like
  a naked
    woman
    I peep
    at you
      Fanta can

I peep
at you new-
    sprouting
  wildflowers
   in new-mowed
   grass
    you'll be blooming in strength
    soon and *then* and *then*
    the butterflies
   will
 come

     *

Listen to
the over-round
 tailpipe's
 maw
   Inhale its holy dirt
     Take back
    this world
    Park your
    butt in
     the
      grass
     and
       stay
        a while
        but don't
       sit *there*
       or *there*

        *

      Stage a sit-
     in with the divine

Embrace a silver fire-
hydrant
          but do not try
          to fuck it
     Embrace a telephone pole
     but do not try to fuck
     it   Climb into an empty
          garbage bin
               and close the
                         lid
                    burst
                    through
                    arms
               to the sky
               and shout
               I've been
          reborn a seed!
          I've sprouted
          from human
               waste
               and
               I've
               come to
               say
               I've seen
          death & no it is
               not
               better

	Steps	Miles	Time	
Feb 10	12882	4.88	1:50	yay!
Feb 11	?	?	?	uh?
Feb 12	7084	2.68	1:03	boo
Feb 13	9845	3.73	1:30	boo
Feb 14	14875	5.64	2:00	yay!
Feb 15	18732	7.10	2:36	yay!
Feb 16	?	?	?	
Feb 17	16030	6.07	2:16	yay!
Feb 18	6973	2.64	1:01	
Feb 19	10694	4.05	1:33	
Feb 20	10434	3.95	1:32	
Feb 21	11465	4.34	1:43	
Feb 22	14497	5.49	2:09	
Feb 23	16298	6.16	2:26	
Feb 24	12654	4.76	1:49	
Feb 25	3737	1.41	33	
Feb 26	?	?	?	
Feb 28	19506	7.39	2:59	
Feb 29				

I'd prefer
not to
upload
my brain
I hope
I can die
while
I still can
spared the
great white
idiots

who've
taken
up the
call of
immortality
and made
a market
venture
out of space
ad and *venture*
the only
2 words
they know

Risky
these
desires
best
to only
listen
to what
the dirt
tells
me

It is factual
in the future
  people will wear
their lovers
on their eyes
  as second eyes
  by which they
   will avoid
    grief entirely
     iCompanion
     iComp
     iCon
     iCo
     will put into
     question the
        integrity
        of all
     physical relationships
    there will
  be several
benefits
+ longer lifespan
+ increased productivity
+ no loneliness
Once iCo is worn over
 one's eyes the wearer
  will not possess the
    willpower to take iCo
      off again
        this device is permanent

Let the
woolly
mammoth
be It
would be
 so   unhappy
  to wake up
   in   a show-
   room   next
   to   a sports car
     and a   newfangled
       watch

Video Game Thoreau
?

Wind-pushed
  swing
  you know
   how stupid
  I am but by
   being stupid
    I am also good
    What good is
    memory if it
      forgets to be
      kind
      What good is
        vocabulary
        if it forgets
        the words
        rock
         mud
          stone

The dog   the whole
holds   walk
a pecan   just to
it its   toss it
mouth   around
                 in the yard
                 with joy
and crunch open
its   contents

Not even Virgil
could navigate
these woods

https://www.irs.gov

When I consider
how my light/ bill
is spent

Requiem
you know
me better now
I go outside
the birds are
horny ornaments
and it's not yet
spring
Patience
it hurts to have
a radio
for a second voice
in the room
Longing
learn to ignore it
notice the age of your
skin what health
means circulation
flowing   big toy
lungs
puffing out
bad behavior
The greatest sound
is consciousness
working its way
through my opposite
ear   Night
Don't be afraid
crisp snail
shells are
glowing outside
they are delicate
they move slowly

please don't move
as slow as them
I can't see myself
with a snail

My future you
    haven't learned
how to abandon
    me yet &
    that's why
    I like you
      There are better
      endeavors than
      mooning over
        an abyss
      I spend my
        time how
        I like
        talking to your
          plate of a face
          singing in your
          vegetable ear
          holding your
          cute twig
          hands
          My future
          our children
          will be likable
            monsters
            I haven't
            grown up
            yet that's
            why I only
            know how
                to kick
                you
                  ouch

Spinoza   or   spermatozoa
     which would
       you prefer
       to go with the sound
       of bells
        the nice
         angels
         are
         ringing
         in the
         towers
       Who cares if
         it's the end
         of the world?
          There's always
           face paint
           and that
           thing you
             do with your hands
              Take for instance
                this grey
                  medieval light
                 isn't it something
                  how cloud cover
                   feels like
                  being in a pot
                  of boiling gruel
                  3 days of rain
                  and I saw
                    a worm
                     a foot 1/2 long
                    almost ran
                    over it

with my
rolling
suitcase
but you made me
see it's
magnificence
pale
pink
corpse
8 worms
in one
a train
chugging
limp on the
wet road
Don't think
I wasn't
thinking it could
afford   to
be separated into thirds
for the sake of
convenience

I almost forgot
to tell you about
the red cardinal
I saw it
pecking at its
image
in the side
mirror
of a parked car
It   flew and came back
flew and came back
to this same image
doubled
of a handsome
red-haired
punk
rabble rouser
narcissus
with red
berry wings

Season: *Spring*

Spring
you came yesterday
  and I didn't
   even throw you
   a party
The birds were
   less raucous today
Who do you think
   you are?!
turning   off and on
   like a hot
    faucet Could it
    be   I was meant
    to be alone
   marrying this green
   giving myself to
    afternoon
    blind to the fact
     that you came yesterday
    and I had other
    things to do
   than watch a baby
    spider as I am
    now getting
    tripped out
    by the wind
    and how
    frustrating life
    can be
    when

it's all food
  and sex food
and sex
  My job might just
   be to rock
    in this chair
   on the front porch
    thinking how I'll
    pack this face
    when I'm older
    the thought that
     creases my brow
    now no different
    from when I
    was a baby
     maybe I don't
     know I shouldn't
     pretend to be a
     philosopher or even
    claim I understand how
    a clock works let alone
     time   Yes let alone
     time
     it can find its
      own mate
     I'll find mine
     in each moment
     I resist making
     myself unhappy

We all get
  older said
  a woman
  on the bus
You think it
  won't happen
  then it does
  She was
  smiling
as she said
this talking
  to some
  kids from
  London
here for a week
   of music
  I take odd
   job after odd job
  living in someone
  else's house
  caring for someone
   else's dog
   in a
  liminal space
  where not
   enough
   rings true
  a big ass gong
   pushing
  forty feeling
  economically
     teen
   I don't need

much &
if sacrifice
means your
love I'd say
it's worth it

The morning
    began
 with   the
 mother
  squirrel
 flashing me
  her   swollen
    teats

An old man
leaning
heavy
on his
crutches
using
the bus
stop
for support
tells
me
to have
a safe
and
blessèd
evening
and
shouts
some
thing
about
belief
and believing
which
I try
to honor
like
the crushed
rose
petals
in
my
book

letter # ?

Spring put
  your pants
  back
  on

Lucky clipboard
Lucky stepometer
Lucky hat
gentle underwear
gentle pants
favorite deodorant
wonky sunglasses
stupid hair tie
feminizing lipstick
pantiliner
pussy smell
neutralizers
mace
lucky rock
but not the
lucky rock
just a sufficiently
lucky rock
comfy shoes
bra
undershirt
tee shirt
over shirt
plaid
various
crumpled
tissues
some new
some hardened
by accidental
washing
water canteen
little journal

and pens
sometimes big
journal
Poems
an umbrella
so it
won't rain

The fig
trees
in the
yard are
showing
their happy
green
testicles

The butterflies
   love my
  lavender scented
    arms and
     hibiscus flavored
     mouth
    They think
   the way
   I dress
  is a mistake
 and that my
  shoes are
   smelly
They wonder
 what happened
  to my nose
 and where
my antenna are
but don't
seem
  concerned
  about how
   much money
  I have
   in my
    pockets

If I knew the name
of every flower
which names
would you prefer
to hear
whispered
which names
would warrant
extra attention
to syllables
jasminum
What if I told
you bottlebrush
is the sort of flower
you'd like to feel
crammed
in your mouth
What if I told you
the perfect temperature
to smell a rose
is 81°
Now that I know
the name of the
yellow butterfly
the Southern
Dogface butterfly
I see it
everywhere
and Mountain
Laurel reminds
me of my sister's
wish
to have

a child
The moment
I smelled a cluster
of laurel
another cluster
was being
visited by a bee
Someone's lawn has
grown two perfect
mushrooms
How do you
respond
to that?

Bright
  Squirrel!

Little
mocking
bird
with your
ladies
fan
tail
and flashy
white
under
feathers
blinding
like
sheets
What
no word?

A poem need never
begin in agony
If it won't have you
trust it will spit
you out of its large
mouth
Till next time

Alright
shut
up mocking
    bird

I hated myself
most of March
        April shoved
    a little brown dove
        down the walk
    she had good posture
        like a dancer
    This made my body
    feel better She was
        caressed by so many
        afternoon shadows
        and seemed to
    like me & I liked
        her   She
            was quiet
            & didn't seem
            to mind
            being alone

Get ready little green
caterpillar
flick

Season: *Summer*

Lords
 Of
Industry
I'm a new
 Dancer
  Articulating
truths like
 pas de chat
I'm not
Confused
I have no
 Company
name my
 Name
 is junkyard
 & I don't
 mind that
 now my
 Deepest
Impulse
 is to make
  a home

in each
Moment
I have
 Spoken
to raging
 Prophets
 & what
they say
 About
the meek
is true
 I've been
preordained
 a happy
basket
 Case
an outsider
Aware
 of temp-
Erature
and light

I see
 good
impulses
and bad
 how the
people
want
their
 green
impossible
grass
 in
 Texas
 &
will
use
chemical
means and
water
to get
 it

Man   I've got   From
don't   a rattle   Your
offer   snake's   Truck
me   tongue   I've
no   &   got 2
ride   limbs   Dusty
I get   like   Angels
where   a jack   On
I'm   rabbit   my side
going   I'd   And
by   caution   the sun
my   you   Purring
soul   against   Through
   spitting   Me
   on   Like
   me   A
      Christ
      Lion

If our only night
together
has to be in hell
fine   I'll take it
that's how much
you move me
beyond what
I think
I know
into
the risk
of
sun
down
& how will
I get home?
This is a good
woods
where I meet
you in my
mind
and rub
my thoughts
against you
like a cat
We don't
need touch
you & I
pink
and
grey
clouds
are enough
touch for me

You met
me on an empty
bus and asked *Which way*
is hell?
And will this
driver take us
there?
I should
have
brought
my
tooth bush
&
gasoline
I should have
robbed a Bank
of America
and given
the angry driver
half
She's speeding
us into
hell
right now
no stops
just pure
sky a cyclone
of clouds
rippling out of
a pink scalloped
edge the eye
of a funnel
opening up
That's how we'll
get there!
Please don't

tease me
with the
possibilities
of
Skyhell
perfectly
polluted
with Texacos
perfectly
inhabited
by evil
& it's evil
to love
you in hell
but that's
why
I do it

I saw a woman
risk her life to
save a little
girl's bright
orange hat
In the return
of this wind-
lifted item
the woman
and the little
girl's mother

embraced in the street
in front of a city
bus that was stopped
at a green light
They embraced
in an intersection
while the light
was green
No one honked
and by some
supreme goodness
the little girl
in the stroller
saw her
mother return

I love life   A woman is on the bus
 pumping   breast milk
  wearing a shirt
  that   says   GO HARD
OR   GO HOME

Flowering
pomegranate
you can wear
your bright
orange   swim
trunks

One day
I'll wag
my cunt
around
like nobody's
business
I'll bathe
in the
sun's
light
and
pinch
parsley
tips
nude
as
a baby
all
my

religion
will leave
me
alone
so I can
call
the sand
and grass
my
new
Gods
I may
be old
& wrinkled
by then
or may-
be
I'll
dare
to scare
wild
rabbits
away to-
morrow

When will
the 29th
bather join
the fun
and nail
the one
she likes
most?

It's easier
for a
bug
to fall
in love
with
you if
you're
wearing
a   white
shirt

no bee
no bee no
bee nooo

—for J. C., who believed in the steps

It's ok to sit
tight with
wildflowers
another friend
exits   this
show Hand
to the sky
it gets
to me
the cynicism
too We have 100
good years left
on this sphere
if we're lucky
so might as well
cut loose
Not like that
Not like he
did

Leaving
his daughter
Behind
The cabbage
butterfly
doesn't care
it does its
own thing
outside
the school
yard where
kids play
and I choke
on my own
heart which
I swear
I can
feel

the warmth
and temperature
of   O kids
O children
there's a drop
off on the other
side of childhood
when you understand
people make
fatal mistakes
They read
the directions
of their
lives wrong
This part
was suppose
to go
there   Maybe
I'll write

Fiction
start getting
the story
I want
In the beginning
there was a handshake
and the animals
said *This*
is what we're
going to do
You humans sit
there &
we'll guide
this boat
Because
clearly you're
incompetent
I love love
Lizards
every time
I see
one I think Frost
What a design
4 inches
Long

colored
stripes down
the back quick
as a minnow
on land
an utter love
of sun
rooted in
affection
for the earth
w/ one's belly
so near
the ground
I can't
toast
to my friend
with any-
thing
but
water
clean
pure
truth
sipped

from a
Magnolia
Leaf

A young man
says good morning
to a porch cat
smoothing
its sun-warm fur

A
girl
lets
go
of her
handle
bars

What the wall
of affection
says:
Dykes
Unite
John
Loves
Kathy
Jon
loves
Jill
KK
+
Bob
+
Bev
No
Holly
wood
Mike
Jim
+
Jo
Teri
Bill
TATE
marry
me?
Amy
loves
Ray
SAD

Dick
RKD
Trio
David
&
Ahn
Shirley
&
Maurice
SWAN
ONCE
FELL
LOVE

Linda
+
Gill
RV
+
VC
Jason T.
I
love
you
Dinky
+
Cathy
+ JP
Gangsta
4
Life
FERNANDAZ

Susie '91
David +
Charity
CRAIG
LOVES
BARBIE
Jon
&
Beatrice
Jinxy
Ferda
was
here
rat kid
Ron
Loves
Tamya
Danny
T
Matt-n-
Allison
Love '89

In the future   I will tell you about
Carolina Wrens
In the future I will tell you about
moss balls
In the future I will tell you about
the green parrots
In the future I will tell you about
I H-35
In the future I will tell you about
the barrel cactus
In the future I will tell you about
the Domain
In the future I will tell you about
my relationship with crows
and blue butterflies
In the future I will tell you what
a grackle is
I will tell you about a particular pair
of running shoes that I can't throw away
and continue to wear for reasons I will
explain in the future
I will explain to you the very curious
juxtaposition of a street named
Robert Browning in an area undergoing
intense development
In the future I hope you can explain to
me certain cryptic features of urban development
In the future I will tell you about
the young man wearing a white
tee shirt that had been signed in sharpie
the words "love you"

and how he wore a rosary backwards
In the future I will tell you about
how often bus drivers have to leave
passengers on the bus to use the facility
How I always wait for someone to commandeer
the bus and drive off but no one ever does
Back from the Texaco the driver carried a
a Red Bull
In the future I will tell you about
my experience teaching poetry to people
with Dementia and early stages of Alzheimer's
I will explain why I quickly took out
the word "suffering"
preceding the word Dementia and early stages
of Alzheimer's
I will tell you about a sign I saw on
a closed down convenience store that said:

MILK BREAD DRUGS

NOTES

p. 21:   Inspired by teaching at the We Are Girls Conference a few days before the 2016 election.

p. 35:   Unicorn Moving and Storage is a company based out of Austin. The sides of the trucks are painted with mural-sized unicorns.

p. 45:   Warhol's iconic *32 Campbell's Soup Cans* and "Warhol Eating a Cheeseburger," taken from the documentary film *66 Scenes from America* by Jørgen Leth.

p. 48   Inefficient stepometer recordkeeping.

p. 49:   Inspired by Elon Musk, owner of Space X, Jeff Bezos, owner of Blue Origin, and Zoltan Istvan, a transhumanist who I learned about in Mark O'Connell's essay "600 Miles in a Coffin-Shaped Bus, Campaigning Against Death Itself" in the *New York Times Magazine*.

p.50:   Inspired by the increasing popularity of VR (Virtual Reality) technology, heavily marketed during the Christmas season 2016.

p. 51:   Inspired by the *New York Times* article "We Might Soon Resurrect Extinct Species. Is it Worth the Cost?" by Steph Yin.

p. 52:   A videogame called *Walden, a game*, released in 2017 by USC Game Innovation Lab.

p. 56:   A nod to Milton's "Sonnet 19."

p. 77:   Inspired by UT Austin campus' "blond" squirrels and Keats's famous love poem.

p. 78:   Northern Mocking Bird.

p. 81:   Mourning dove.

p. 85:   *Pas de Chat* is a ballet term meaning "step of the cat."

p. 94:   Inspired by Whitman's "Song of Myself, IX."

p. 98:   Points to Frost's poem "Design." Could not properly identify lizard.

p. 101:   Inspired by love notes carved into stone on UT's campus.

Acknowledgments

I would like to thank CapMetro, Austin's public transportation system, for pushing me to use my legs to get around. I would like to thank my East Austin neighborhood for being the inspiration for many of these poems. I would like to thank green anoles, worms, snakes, lizards I could not identify, frogs, toads, blue jays, mockingbirds, robins, Carolina Wrens, tufted titmice, cedar waxwings, mourning doves, grackles, great blue herons, green herons, red-shouldered hawks, cardinals, and monk parakeets. I would like to thank butterflies and moths as well as numerous bugs. I would like to thank all those who plant roses in their front yard. And I would like to give a special shoutout to neighborhood cats.

To Dean Young and Noelle Kocot for reading the first iteration of this manuscript. Thank you both for telling me to keep going when I asked what I should do next.

To Malvern Books and all my amazing coworkers. I'm so fortunate that I got to participate in Joe Bratcher's vision. Malvern will go down in history as one of the best bookstores in the world.

To my Texas friends Taisia Kitaiskaia, Fernando A. Flores, Alysia Nicole Harris, Claire Bowman, Annar Veröld, Austin Rodenbiker, Katelin Kelly, Leti Bueno, and Stephanie Goehring. I'm consistently in awe of your talent. To my friends and family in the great Pacific Northwest.

Special thanks to virtual groups such as the Writer's League of Texas and Typewriter Tarot for providing the space and motivation to write.

Last, but not least, to Deep Vellum. I'm deeply fortunate to have worked with poetry editor and poet Sebastián Páramo. Thank you Sebastián for your kindness and encouragement during the editing process. To Sara Balabanlilar and Walker Rutter-Bowman for helping someone with no social media presence connect with readers. Thank you Linda Stack-Nelson from protecting people against my unintentional typos. Thank you to Kirkby Gann Tittle and cover design by Zoe Novell. My heartfelt gratitude to Will Evans for supporting my work; you are a visionary.

Lastly, thank you to my future soul mate for inspiring these poems. If you're out there, drop me a text.

Biographical Information

Julie Poole is a poet, journalist, and filmmaker based in Austin. She received a B.A. from Columbia University and an M.F.A. from the New Writers Project at the University of Texas. She has received fellowship and grant support from the James A. Michener Center, the Economic Hardship Reporting Project, and the PEN Writers Fund. She has been a resident at the Helene Wurlitzer Foundation, the Corsicana Artist and Writer Residency, and Yaddo. Her first book of poems, *Bright Specimen*, was inspired by the Billie L. Turner Plant Resources Center at UT.